Orang-utan Baby

by Monica Hughes

Editorial consultant: Mitch Cronick

Copyright © **ticktock Entertainment Ltd 2006**
First published in Great Britain in 2006 by **ticktock Media Ltd.,**
Unit 2, Orchard Business Centre, North Farm Road, Tunbridge Wells, Kent TN2 3XF

We would like to thank: Shirley Bickler and Suzanne Baker

ISBN 1 86007 974 1 pbk
Printed in China

Picture credits
t=top, b=bottom, c=centre, l-left, r=right, OFC= outside front cover
All images courtesy of Digital Vision

Every effort has been made to trace the copyright holders, and we apologise in advance for any unintentional omissions. We would be pleased to insert the appropriate acknowledgements in any subsequent edition of this publication.

CONTENTS

What is an orang-utan?

An orang-utan is a big ape.

Orang-utans live in rainforests in Asia.

Orang-utan

Asia

Orang-utans
live here

World map

4

Other apes

Gorilla

Gibbon

Chimpanzee

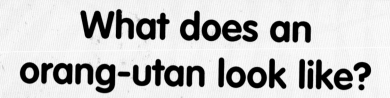

What does an orang-utan look like?

An orang-utan has long orange hair.

An orang-utan has long arms.

6

A mother orang-utan

The father orang-utan is very big.

A father orang-utan

Meet a baby orang-utan

This is a baby orang-utan with his mother.

They live in the trees.

They do not live with the
father orang-utan.

9

What does the baby orang-utan eat?

The baby orang-utan
eats fruit.

His mother chews the fruit.

She makes the fruit soft.

Then she gives it to the baby.

The baby drinks his mother's
milk too.

Orang-utan food

When the baby is bigger he gets his own food.

He eats fruit and leaves.

He eats ants and snails and eggs too.

Fruit

Ants

Snails

How does the baby get about?

The mother orang-utan has long hair.

The baby holds on to her long hair.

The baby holds on when
she swings from tree to tree.

When does the baby go off on his own?

When the baby gets bigger he goes off on his own.

He holds on to the branches.

He swings from tree to tree.

Making a nest

The baby orang-utan sleeps
with his mother at night.

His mother makes a nest in
the trees.

She makes the nest from leaves.

Orang-utans in danger

Orang-utans live in the trees in a rainforest.

The trees in a rainforest can be cut down.

If all the trees are cut down where will the orang-utans live?

21

Yes or no?
Talking about orang-utans

Orang-utans live
in a rainforest.

Yes or no?

The baby orang-utan lives
with his father.

22

Yes or no?

The baby orang-utan
eats fruit and leaves.

Yes or no?

The baby orang-utan
holds on to his mother.

Yes or no?

The baby orang-utan sleeps
in a bed.

Yes or no?

Activities

What did you think of this book?

 Brilliant   **Good**   **OK**

Which page did you like best? Why?

• • • • • • • • • • • • • • •

Make a big poster to show that orang-utans are in danger.

• • • • • • • • • • • • • • •

Who is the author of this book? Have you read *Tiger Cub* by the same author?

• • • • • • • • • • • • • • •

Look at the picture of the orang-utan's hand. How is it like your hand?